CHESTER A. *Arthur*

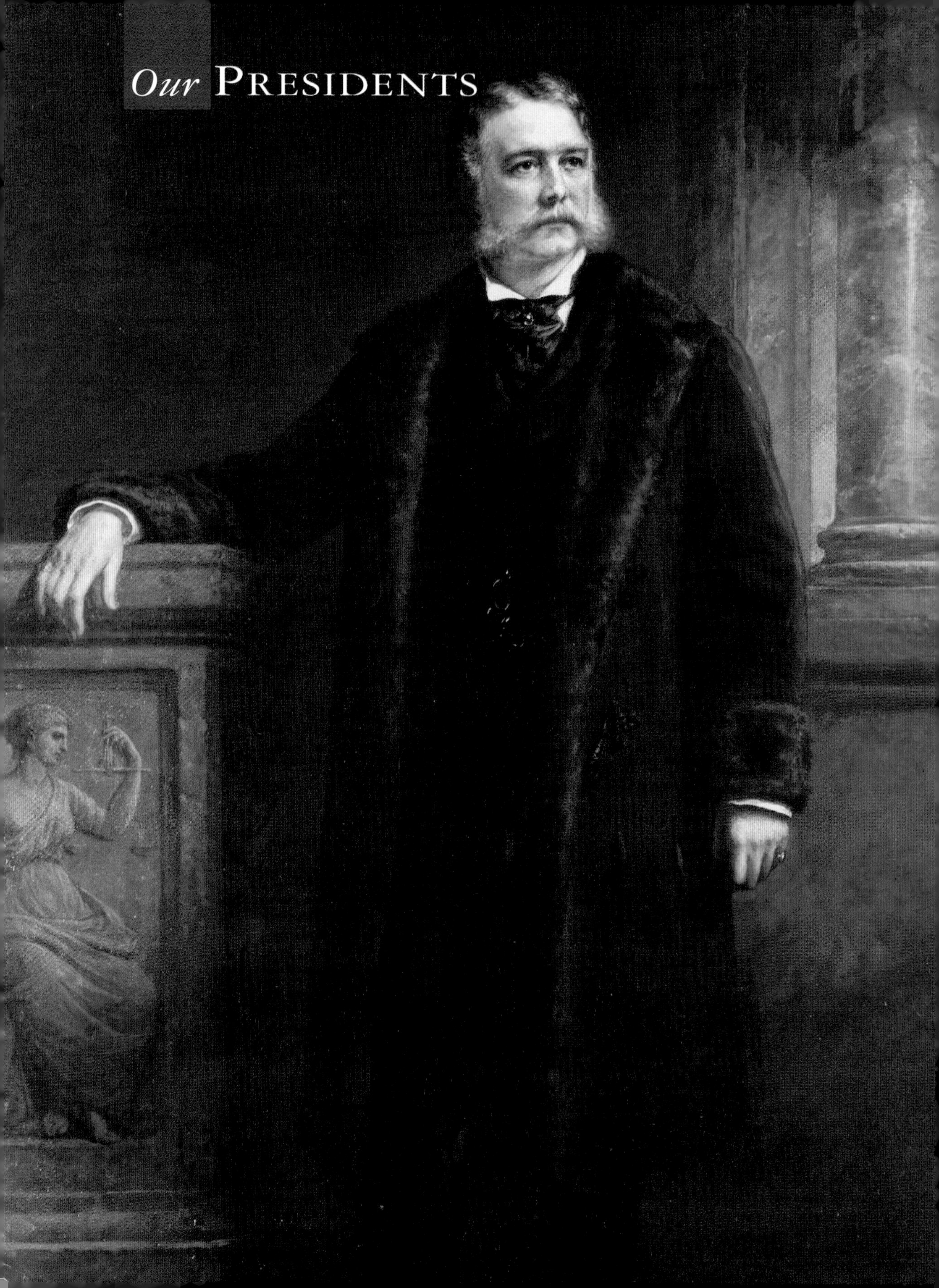
Our PRESIDENTS

CHESTER A. *Arthur*

OUR TWENTY-FIRST PRESIDENT

By Carol Brunelli

SPIRIT
of America™

The Child's World®, Inc.
Chanhassen, Minnesota

7

CHESTER A. *Arthur*

Published in the United States of America by The Child's World®, Inc.
PO Box 326 • Chanhassen, MN 55317-0326 • 800-599-READ • www.childsworld.com

Acknowledgments
The Creative Spark: Mary Francis-DeMarois, Project Director; Elizabeth Sirimarco Budd, Series Editor; Robert Court, Design and Art Direction; Janine Graham, Page Layout; Jennifer Moyers, Production

The Child's World®, Inc.: Mary Berendes, Publishing Director; Red Line Editorial, Fact Research; Cindy Klingel, Curriculum Advisor; Robert Noyed, Historical Advisor

Photos
Cover, 20, 31: White House Collection, courtesy White House Historical Association; Bettmann/Corbis: 15; The Library of Congress: 8, 10, 12, 13, 14, 17, 18, 21, 23, 24, 27, 29, 32, 33, 34, 36, 37; National Portrait Gallery, Smithsonian Institute, Art Resource, NY: 25; North Wind Picture Archives: 28, 30; Courtesy of Union College, Schaffer Library, Schenectady, NY: 6, 9; Vermont Division for Historic Preservation, President Chester A. Arthur State Historic Site: 7

Library of Congress Cataloging-in-Publication Data
Brunelli, Carol.
    Chester A. Arthur, our twenty-first president / by Carol Brunelli.
      p. cm.
    Includes bibliographical references and index.
    ISBN 1-56766-858-5 (lib. bdg. : alk. paper)
    1. Arthur, Chester Alan, 1829–1886—Juvenile literature. 2. Presidents—United States—
Biography—Juvenile literature. [1. Arthur, Chester Alan, 1829–1886. 2. Presidents.] I. Title.
    E692 .B78 2001
    973.8'4'092—dc21
                                                                    00-010944

22   33   37

Contents

Chapter ONE	Abolitionist and Lawyer	6
Chapter TWO	Political Leader of New York City	14
Chapter THREE	An Honest President	24
Chapter FOUR	Father of the U.S. Navy	32
	Time Line	38
	Glossary Terms	40
	Our Presidents	42
	Presidential Facts	46
	For Further Information	47
	Index	48

Abolitionist and Lawyer

Chester Arthur became the president in 1881 after the death of the elected president, James Garfield.

CHESTER ALAN ARTHUR, THE 21ST U.S. president, was not the only president to come from Vermont. Calvin Coolidge, the 30th president, was also from the "Green Mountain State." Although Arthur was born more than 40 years before Coolidge, the two men had many things in common. Both grew up in small Vermont farming communities. Both were Republicans, which means they were members of one of the country's most powerful political parties. Political parties are groups of people who share similar ideas about how to run the government. Both Arthur and Coolidge were elected vice president. And, as vice president, both men rose to the presidency after the president died. Arthur became president after the death of

James Garfield in 1881. Coolidge became president after the death of Warren Harding in 1923.

Arthur's father, William, came from Ireland. He moved to Canada as a young man. Soon William began working as a schoolteacher in a village near the Vermont border. He met 18-year-old Malvina Stone, whose family came from Vermont and New Hampshire. In 1821, the young couple married.

The Arthurs and their five children lived in a small house when their first son, Chester, was a baby. The house at left was built by the state of Vermont in 1953. It is a copy of the home where the Arthur family moved in 1830. The photograph at right, taken in 1880, shows the actual building where they lived. Builders used the photograph to create the new house.

William Arthur (Chester's father) was born on December 5, 1796, in Cullybackey, Ireland. He moved to North America with other members of his family between 1816 and 1820. There he met and married Malvina Stone and eventually earned his living as a Baptist minister.

The growing Arthur family lived in many Vermont towns, where William taught school. He also studied to become a lawyer. Finally, he decided he wanted to become a minister. By 1828, one year before Chester was born, William was the pastor of a small church in North Fairfield, Vermont. On October 5, 1829, Chester was born, the fifth of William and Malvina's nine children. The Arthur family moved several more times within Vermont before they went to New York State in 1835. That year, William Arthur helped start the New York Anti-Slavery Society. Both William and Malvina were religious people. They had strong feelings about what was right and wrong and believed all human beings were created equal. They said that all people deserved to be treated with respect. Because of this, they fought to end slavery in the United States. At the time, Americans who wanted to end, or abolish, slavery were called abolitionists.

The Arthurs moved to Saratoga County, New York, in 1839. William Arthur continued his work as a minister. This gave him a chance to share his anti-slavery beliefs with the people who came to his services. Chester grew up hating slavery. He held many of his parents' strong opinions. After he became interested in **politics,** he would have the chance to share his beliefs with others.

In 1845, Chester was ready to attend college. He enrolled at Union College in Schenectady, New York. He was a friendly

and outgoing young man, and other students liked him. He was tall, social, and good looking. In 1848, Chester graduated and decided to study law. To help pay for his studies, he worked as a schoolteacher. In 1851, he became the principal of a school that met in the basement of his father's church in North Pownal, Vermont.

In 1853, Chester moved to New York City to work for a friend of his father, Erastus D.

Like his parents, Arthur opposed slavery and wanted to see it made illegal in the United States. As a lawyer, he worked to help African Americans gain better treatment and win their freedom.

Culver. The following year, he attended the Anti-Nebraska Convention in Saratoga Springs. The purpose of this large meeting was to **protest** the Kansas-Nebraska Act. Many feared this new law would increase the places in the United States where slavery was legal. More and more, there were problems between the northern and southern states because of slavery. Many Northerners wanted to stop it. But people in the South did not think they could run their large farms if slavery were abolished. When the Kansas-Nebraska Act made it possible for new slave states to enter the **Union,** many abolitionists— including Chester Arthur—were furious.

At the Anti-Nebraska Convention, people joined together to form the Republican Party of New York State. This new political party was formed in part to fight the spread of slavery into new **territories.** That same year, Arthur passed his law exams. He went to work in Erastus Culver's firm and quickly became known as a supporter of **civil rights** for blacks. First, Arthur helped defend Lizzie Jennings, an African American who was forced off a streetcar that was reserved for

Arthur became a well-known lawyer in New York, praised for his work helping African Americans win their freedom.

white people only. Arthur won $250 in the lawsuit for Jennings, which was a lot of money at the time. Because of this win, African Americans were guaranteed the right to ride on any streetcar in New York City.

Arthur also helped Culver win another civil rights case. A man named Jonathan Lemmon brought eight slaves from the Southern state of Virginia with him to New York. Slavery was legal in Virginia, but it was against the law in New York. The slaves wanted their freedom. Arthur and Culver fought for them in court. Judge Elijah Paine of New York ruled in favor of the slaves, saying that because they had come to a free state, they were now free.

The Lemmon case made Arthur famous in New York City. In 1856, he opened his own law office. He also worked for the **campaign** of John C. Fremont, the Republican **candidate** for president. From that time forward, Arthur was an active member of the Republican Party.

TODAY'S REPUBLICAN PARTY WAS FORMED during the 1850s. At the time, the issue of slavery was threatening to divide the nation. The two most powerful political parties, the Whigs and the Democrats, were divided on the issue as well. The Whigs wanted to abolish slavery. Democrats wanted to protect it. Some people were not satisfied with either political party. They began talking about forming a new one.

A man named Alan Earl Bovay was one of the founders of the Republican Party. He believed the new party should fight slavery and represent other interests of the North. He called the party "Republican" because the word describes a place where all citizens have equal rights. Years before, Thomas Jefferson had chosen "Republican" to refer to his party, the Democratic-Republican Party. Later, that party became known simply as the Democratic Party.

In 1854, Chester Arthur went to the Anti-Nebraska Convention in Saratoga Springs, New York. The purpose of this meeting was to protest the Kansas-Nebraska Act. This act increased tensions between the North and the South because it made it possible to add new slave-holding states to the Union. The people attending the convention created the New York Republican Party, which was against the expansion of slave-holding territory.

In 1856, Arthur worked on the campaign of the first Republican presidential candidate, John Fremont. Although the party lost the election to the Democrats, it won a third of the total vote. By 1860, the Republican Party had gained strength. Its candidate, Abraham Lincoln, won the election that year, making him the first Republican president.

Chapter TWO

Political Leader of New York City

Arthur met his future wife, Ellen Herndon, in 1856. She was from Virginia and was the daughter of a naval officer.

ARTHUR BECAME A WELL-KNOWN LAWYER IN New York City, and he would soon become a well-known politician. He was tall with black eyes and brown hair, rosy red cheeks, and a high forehead. He went to the best tailors and always wore stylish clothing. People enjoyed his company, and he was considered well read and amusing.

One day in 1856, he met a lovely young woman, the cousin of one of his roommates. Her name was Ellen Herndon, and she was visiting from her home in Virginia. Chester and Ellen were fond of each other from the beginning, and they soon fell in love. They married in October of 1859. The Arthurs had a daughter, Ellen, and a son, Chester Alan Jr.

In 1860, Arthur campaigned in New York City for the Republican presidential candidate, Abraham Lincoln. Arthur also worked hard for the reelection of Edwin D. Morgan, the governor of New York. When Morgan won, Arthur was given an important job in the state government.

Arthur found success as a young lawyer in New York City. He soon became involved in politics and became well known in the city.

Tensions between the North and South continued to grow more serious, and it seemed that war could not be avoided. The **Civil War** began in 1861. President Lincoln put Governor Morgan in charge of New York's volunteer soldiers. The state had to supply the soldiers with clothing, food, equipment, and shelter. Morgan named Arthur inspector general and then quartermaster general of the state armies. As the quartermaster general, Arthur was in charge of making sure the troops had all the supplies they needed. He held the position until 1863, when Democrat Horatio Seymour was elected governor of New York.

When Seymour replaced Governor Morgan in 1863, Arthur returned to his law practice. But he stayed in close contact with the city's Republican Party. The boss, or leader, of the party in New York was Senator Roscoe Conkling. Arthur supported Conkling and became one of his most important assistants.

Conkling and his followers were called Stalwarts. The Stalwarts were a small **faction** within the party. Even though they were Republicans, they did not always agree with other people in the party. In 1868, the

16

During the first two years of the American Civil War, Arthur was the quartermaster general of New York State. He was in charge of organizing food and supplies for U.S. soldiers.

17

The Customhouse of New York, shown here, was the largest government office in the nation, with more than 1,000 employees. As the collector of customs, Arthur was in charge of its operations. He met many important Republican leaders while he held the position.

Stalwarts supported General Ulysses S. Grant as the Republican candidate for president, and he won the election. President Grant wanted to reward the people who had helped him win the election. This included Arthur, who was a loyal Stalwart Republican. In 1871, Grant **appointed** him to a powerful position, the collector of customs at the New York Customhouse. Arthur was in charge of the entire office.

18

The customs collector was an important political position. Arthur oversaw the movement of all goods into the busy New York harbor. He collected taxes charged on all items brought from other countries to sell in the United States. The position was so powerful that Arthur became the leader of the party in New York City. He was also the chairman of the Republican state committee.

Arthur used his new power to make the Republican Party stronger. He gave jobs to many members of the party. In fact, he gave Senator Conkling's followers, the Stalwarts, many positions at the customhouse. Although Arthur was an honest man, he gave too many jobs to the Stalwarts. These people worked hard for the election of Republicans, but they did not work very hard at the customhouse. Some people were angry that these men were paid to help the Republican Party, not to do their jobs.

In 1877, Rutherford B. Hayes became president. He was a Republican, but he did not like the Stalwarts. He later fired Arthur from the position of collector. President Hayes said Arthur had used the government's money

to reward his political supporters. Arthur did have connections with many of the powerful New York politicians of the time, but no one ever proved that he had done something wrong. Hayes soon hired one of his own supporters as the collector of customs. After

Arthur was fired, some Americans were angry. They thought Hayes had treated him unfairly. Many Republicans still supported Arthur.

In 1880, it was time for the Republicans to choose a candidate for the next presidential election. At first, they could not come to a decision. After some time, they made a **compromise.** They **nominated** James Garfield of Ohio as their candidate for president. They chose Arthur as their candidate for vice president. They hoped his fame in the important state of New York would win votes for the party. Senator Conkling did not like James Garfield. In fact, he told Arthur to turn down the nomination, saying, "Drop it as you would a red hot shoe from the forge." Arthur refused to do so. "The office of the vice president is a greater honor than I ever dreamed of attaining," he said.

Unfortunately, 1880 was not a happy year for Arthur, even though he won the nomination. His wife caught a cold that grew very serious. Arthur was out of town when he heard of her illness. He caught a train immediately but could not reach home before Ellen lost consciousness. He stayed by

21

her bedside for 24 hours, hoping she would wake. Sadly, she died the next day at the age of 42. Deeply saddened, Arthur felt guilty for having spent so much time away from home, pursuing his career. "Honors to me," he said, "are not what they once were."

OUR NATION'S CHOICE.

HARMONY, PEACE AND PROSPERITY.

OUR NATION'S HONOR WILL BE PRESERVED.

Gen. JAMES ABRAM GARFIELD, Republican Candidate for President.

Gen. CHESTER A. ARTHUR, Republican Candidate for Vice-President.

ANOTHER PRESIDENT WHO HAD A RISE IN THE WORLD.

IN U.S. HISTORY, A Stalwart was a member of a faction within the Republican Party. Although President Rutherford B. Hayes was a Republican, he did not like the Stalwarts. For one thing, he was against the system of patronage, the practice of giving government jobs to loyal supporters of the Republican Party. He wanted to create a "merit system," which would give jobs to people who were qualified, not to the friends of politicians. The Stalwarts did not like what Hayes was doing. They had gained a great deal of power through the patronage system.

When President Hayes fired Stalwart Chester Arthur from his position as collector of customs, Arthur worried it might hurt his career in politics. He thought that people might believe he had done something wrong. But the Stalwarts still supported him, and his career continued. In fact, just two years later, the Republicans selected Arthur as their vice presidential candidate.

This political cartoon shows Arthur being kicked out of the customhouse after President Hayes fired him. When Arthur ran for vice president, some of his enemies reminded voters about the incident. They hoped it would help Democrats win the election. But the plan failed, and Garfield and Arthur entered office in 1881.

Chapter THREE

An Honest President

Americans believed James Garfield would make a good president. Unfortunately, he had little time to achieve his goals. He was killed during the first year of his presidency.

IN THE 1880 CAMPAIGN, THE DEMOCRATS attacked Arthur's record as customs collector. They reminded people that he had been fired from the position. They also said negative things about his friendship with Conkling and the Stalwart Republicans. The election was close, but Garfield and Arthur won. Arthur was sworn in as vice president on March 4, 1881.

After the election, the question of patronage became a problem. Patronage is the act of giving people government jobs in exchange for their loyalty to a party. Party leaders worked hard to get good jobs for their friends and supporters. This practice often allowed people who were not qualified to hold positions of responsibility that paid excellent wages. Other people who might do the job better, but who had differing views, were out of luck. In exchange for a job, some people were even forced to give part of their wages to the political party.

Conkling wanted President Garfield to find jobs for loyal Republicans in New York State, especially those from the Stalwart faction. He also wanted the president to ask his advice about who should get these jobs. Arthur agreed with Conkling, who had always supported him in the past. At first, Garfield tried to reach a compromise and give Conkling part of what he wanted. But Conkling wanted all or nothing. He believed every position should go to Republican Stalwarts. The president firmly refused to go along with him. Finally, Conkling left his seat in the Senate. People respected Garfield for standing up to the powerful Republican faction, but he had made enemies as well.

Arthur was pleased to be the vice president, but he had no way of knowing that he would soon be forced to take over the office of chief executive.

25

On July 2, 1881, soon after Conkling left the Senate, a mentally ill man named Charles J. Guiteau shot President Garfield. As Guiteau fired the gun, he declared, "I did it and will go to jail for it. I am a Stalwart, and Arthur is president now." Some people took this to mean that Arthur had something to do with the incident. It was soon proven that this was not the case. But Arthur was hurt by such terrible words and by suggestions that he take over the presidency while Garfield was still alive. "I am overwhelmed with grief. The most frightful responsibility … would be casting the presidency on me."

President Garfield lingered at death's door for nearly 80 days. On September 19, 1881, he died. The following morning, Arthur took the oath of office from his home in New York City. He did not make a formal speech, but he did say a few words: "No higher or more assuring proof could exist of the strength and permanence of popular government than the fact that though the chosen of the people be struck down, his … successor is peacefully installed without shock or strain." Arthur was talking about President Garfield's death.

Charles J. Guiteau had made plans to kill President Garfield once before. He even followed him into the Washington train station but then decided not to shoot. Less than one month later, he followed Garfield into the train station again. But this time, he fired two fatal shots.

He reminded Americans that their government was still strong and that it would continue to serve them even if their elected president died.

Arthur was well qualified to be president. After all, he had held important government positions in New York. As a lawyer, he knew the law and the U.S. **Constitution** well. But would Arthur be an honest president? Or would he give jobs to people who cooperated with Conkling and the Stalwarts?

When Garfield was president, Arthur wanted him to give jobs to Conkling's friends and supporters. But as president, Arthur was determined to be a good leader. He wanted to

Interesting Facts

▶ Garfield and Arthur's secretary of war was Robert T. Lincoln, the son of President Abraham Lincoln.

▶ Arthur tried to help Native Americans by protecting their land from settlers who were claiming the land as their own. Unfortunately, his efforts failed.

When Arthur heard the news of President Garfield's death, he wept. "It cannot be," he said. "I do hope it is a mistake." The following morning, he took the oath of office to become the 21st president.

go down in history as an honest and admired man. He tried to follow Garfield's ideals.

Many Americans thought Arthur would be Conkling's puppet, which means they thought he would do whatever Conkling said. But Arthur was an independent president. He tried to work with all members of the Republican Party, not just the Stalwarts. He also worked with members of the other powerful political party, the Democrats. He avoided his old political friends and tried to carry out President Garfield's plans for an honest government.

Arthur continued what Garfield had started in two important ways. First, he completed an investigation of dishonesty within the U.S. Postal Service. Star routes were private postal routes that brought mail to places without regular delivery. Some of the people who ran the routes charged more for the service than they should have. Some even charged for services they did not provide. One of Arthur's political friends played a role

in the Star Route **scandal.**
Even so, Arthur and his assistants worked to put an end
to the dishonesty at the
Postal Service.

The second way Arthur
tried to carry out Garfield's
plans was to support the
merit system. He wanted
people to receive government
jobs because of their skills,
not because of their loyalty to
a party. Many jobs were
available in the Treasury

Department. At first, Americans were sure
Arthur would give most of the positions to
Stalwarts. But Arthur appointed them to only
a few positions.

Starting in 1882, Arthur supported a **bill**
called the Pendleton Act. Once passed, this
new law created the Civil Service Commission.
This organization required that people take
tests for many government jobs. The people
who scored highest on the tests received the
positions. The act also made it illegal for a
political party to take money from govern-

*This political cartoon
shows Thomas Brady,
Garfield and Arthur's
adviser, holding a bag of
stars that symbolize the
Postal Service Star Routes.
Arthur was disappointed
to learn that one of his
friends was involved in
dishonest activities.*

In this cartoon, seven politicians look at Chester Arthur, wondering if he will be a good president. Portraits of Millard Fillmore, John Tyler, and Andrew Johnson are hung on the wall. Like Arthur, these three presidents had entered office after the elected president died. But none of them were successful. An empty frame waits for Arthur's portrait. Fortunately, Arthur proved that he was fit for the job. He became known as an honest president.

ment employees. Many of Arthur's followers turned against him when he signed this act.

During his presidency, there were almost equal numbers of Democrats and Republicans in Congress. It was difficult for Arthur to get bills passed because there were so many different ideas about how to run the government. It seemed as if members of Congress were too busy fighting with each other to make laws that would help the country. Fortunately, the American public approved of the Pendleton Act, so Congress agreed to pass it. Arthur signed the bill into law on January 16, 1883.

30

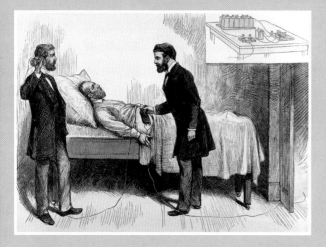

JAMES GARFIELD LIVED FOR MORE than two months after he was shot. Doctors tried many times to take out the bullet that was lodged in his chest, but they couldn't find it. Two scientists, Simon Newcomb and Alexander Graham Bell, tried to help. Newcomb was working on running electricity through wire coils. He found that when metal was placed near the coils, he could hear a faint hum. He hoped to perfect his invention so that it could be used to locate the bullet.

Bell read about Newcomb in a newspaper. He offered his help, suggesting that his invention, the telephone, might be able to improve Newcomb's invention. It could make the humming sound louder. The two men joined forces and came up with an early version of a metal detector.

On July 26, Bell and Newcomb went to the White House to try their invention. The detector made a humming sound no matter where it was placed on the president's body. Bell and Newcomb left the White House confused and disappointed. Why didn't their invention work?

Bell returned to the lab with Newcomb. They ran more experiments, and their invention worked well. They returned to the White House on the last day of July. The same thing happened again. No matter where they placed the detector on the president's body, a faint hum could be heard.

What was wrong with Bell and Newcomb's invention? The invention wasn't the problem. The problem was the president's bed! It had springs made of metal, so the metal detector kept humming and humming. The White House was one of the few places that had mattresses with metal springs at the time. If Bell and Newcomb had moved the president off the bed and onto the floor, their invention could have found the bullet. James Garfield might have lived!

Chapter FOUR

Father of the U.S. Navy

Aside from his honesty, President Chester A. Arthur became well known for being the most elegant and best-dressed president. He had about 80 suits in his closet.

THE U.S. NAVY HAD BEEN AMONG THE strongest in the world during the Civil War. But by the 1880s, it was one of the weakest. Every major European nation, as well as several Latin American countries, had better navies than the United States. The U.S. Navy was in a poor position to protect the country. If a war broke out, it was not prepared.

President Arthur decided that the United States needed to rebuild its navy. He had members of his **cabinet** make suggestions to improve it. These ideas became part of the Navy Bill. The main purpose of the bill was to construct 68 new steel ships. At the time, the navy's ships were made of wood.

After a long debate, Congress agreed to the construction of a few steel ships. In 1885, before Arthur left office, Congress agreed to build four more. The first four ships that were built were called the ABCD ships because they were named the Atlanta, the Boston, the Chicago, and the Dolphin. Another result of the Navy Bill was the creation of the Naval War College in Newport, Rhode Island.

The passage of the Navy Bill was a first step toward making the United States a major naval power. Arthur earned great respect from the U.S. Navy for his efforts, but it was not until the 1890s that America's first battleships were built. Arthur did not have enough support from Congress to achieve his goals.

Although Arthur was a good president, some people thought he did not spend enough time on the job. He is shown in this political cartoon (seated in center) with his cabinet members, the men who helped him make important decisions. Although they should be talking about important issues, they are shown asleep on the job, without having made any decisions.

President Arthur took advantage of any spare time he could find. He loved to take vacations and is shown here during a trip to Newport, Rhode Island. "I need a holiday as much as the poorest of my fellow citizens," he once said. "But it is generally supposed that we people at Washington do not want any rest."

Arthur also disagreed with Congress on the Chinese Exclusion Act. Originally, this bill intended to keep Chinese people from **immigrating** to the United States for 20 years. It also would have denied citizenship to U.S. residents of Chinese ancestry. Arthur decided to **veto** the bill, for he still believed in civil rights. But some Americans claimed that the Chinese were taking away too many jobs, especially in the West. Congress was determined to pass the bill. Arthur finally signed a different version that limited Chinese immigration for 10 years instead of 20. Unfortunately, it also denied citizenship to Chinese people who had lived in the United States for many years. The act was in force until 1943.

Arthur and members of Congress continued to disagree throughout his **term** as president. Congress proposed a bill to spend $19 million to improve rivers and harbors, especially those in the South. Arthur thought this was a waste of money and vetoed it. Congress rejected his veto and approved it. Even though he lost this fight and several others, Americans respected President Arthur for taking a stand.

Arthur did not gain the support of Congress during his **administration,** but he did gain the approval of the American public. Many people who once criticized him were now his supporters. Writer Mark Twain complimented Arthur, saying, "I am but one in 55,000,000; still, in the opinion of this one-fifty-five millionth of the country's population, it would be hard to better President Arthur's administration. But don't decide till you hear from the rest."

While he was president, Arthur learned that he was suffering from Bright's disease,

Few people knew it, but President Arthur's health was failing. He suffered from a kidney disease that could not be cured. It made the responsibility of being president all the more difficult, and he did not try to win the Republican nomination in 1884.

a kidney ailment that did not have a cure. Arthur did not want to tell the American public for fear that they would lose faith in him. For a while, he thought about running for a second term as president, but this was not to be. In private, he told his son that he simply did not feel well enough to handle the duties of president for four more years.

Arthur did not try to win the Republican nomination for president in 1884. In the end, the party chose James G. Blaine as their candidate. At the end of Arthur's term, he returned to his home in New York. Nearly two years later, on November 18, 1886, he died of Bright's disease.

As president, Chester Arthur proved that he had a mind of his own. He also proved that he did not work for a political party, but for all Americans. He gave the country an honest administration. He helped rebuild the U.S. Navy. By the end of his presidency, Arthur had won the respect of American citizens. As one writer explained it, "No man ever entered the presidency so profoundly and widely distrusted, and no one ever retired ... more generally respected."

THE GREAT NATIONAL FISHING MATCH.

IT'S MINE?

"THE RESULT."

In the election of 1884, James Blaine ran against Grover Cleveland. This cartoon shows Cleveland as a fisherman, "landing" the presidency as a disappointed Blaine looks on. Cleveland won the election and became president in 1885.

1821 William and Malvina Arthur, Chester's parents, are married.

1828 William Arthur studies to become a Baptist minister. He becomes the pastor of a church in North Fairfield, Vermont.

1829 Chester Arthur is born on October 5 in North Fairfield.

1835 The Arthurs move to New York State. William Arthur helps start the New York Anti-Slavery Society.

1839 The Arthur family moves to Saratoga County, New York.

1845 Arthur enrolls at Union College in Schenectady, New York.

1848 Arthur graduates from Union College. He begins studying law and working as a schoolteacher.

1851 Arthur becomes the principal of a school in the basement of his father's church in North Pownal, Vermont.

1853 Arthur moves to New York City to work for Erastus D. Culver.

1854 Arthur begins practicing law in New York City.

1855 Arthur defends Lizzie Jennings, who was forced off a streetcar because she was black. The judge decides that blacks must be allowed to use public transportation in New York. Arthur also works with Erastus Culver on the Lemmon case, which determines that slaves who travel into the state of New York are considered free.

1859 Arthur marries Ellen Lewis Herndon in October.

1860 Arthur campaigns for two Republican candidates: Edwin D. Morgan for governor of New York and Abraham Lincoln for U.S. president. Both candidates win their elections.

1861 The American Civil War begins. Arthur is named inspector general and then quartermaster general of New York. His job is to make sure that soldiers have enough food and supplies.

1863 Arthur resigns from his position as quartermaster general. He returns to his law practice and begins a political friendship with Roscoe Conkling of the Stalwart faction.

1865 The Civil War ends.

1868 Arthur and the Stalwarts support General Ulysses S. Grant in the presidential election.

1871 President Ulysses S. Grant appoints Arthur collector of customs at the New York Customhouse.

1878 President Rutherford B. Hayes fires Arthur from his position at the New York Customhouse.

1880 Ellen Arthur dies. Arthur becomes the Republican candidate for vice president.

1881 Garfield is inaugurated on March 4. He dies on September 19, less than 200 days after taking office. Vice President Arthur becomes the 21st president.

1882 The Chinese Exclusion Act passes, stopping Chinese people from immigrating to the United States for 10 years. Arthur does not support this legislation. He learns that he is suffering from Bright's disease.

1883 Arthur signs the Pendleton Civil Service Act, the nation's first civil service law, which requires people to pass a test to get a government job. It also makes it illegal to require that employees give part of their salary to support a political campaign.

1884 Congress votes to replace some of the U.S. Navy's wooden ships with steel ones. Arthur gains nickname "Father of the U.S. Navy." He does not actively seek to win the Republican nomination as its presidential candidate. The Republicans select James Blaine, who loses the election to Grover Cleveland.

1885 Arthur moves back to New York.

1886 Arthur dies on November 18 at age 57.

administration (ad-min-ih-STRAY-shun)
An administration is the period of time that a president holds office. Arthur did not gain the support of Congress during his administration.

appointed (uh-POINT-ed)
If someone is appointed to a position, he or she is asked by an important official to accept the position. President Grant appointed Arthur collector of customs.

bill (BILL)
A bill is an idea for a new law that is presented to a group of lawmakers. Arthur supported a bill called the Pendleton Act.

cabinet (KAB-ih-net)
A cabinet is the group of people who advise a president. Members of Arthur's cabinet made suggestions to improve the navy.

campaign (kam-PAYN)
A campaign is the process of running for an election, including activities such as giving speeches or attending rallies. Arthur worked on the campaigns of Republican candidates.

candidate (KAN-dih-det)
A candidate is a person running in an election. Arthur campaigned for the first Republican candidate for president, John Fremont.

civil rights (SIV-il RYTZ)
Civil rights are the rights granted to citizens of the United States by the Constitution. As a lawyer, Arthur protected the civil rights of blacks.

civil war (SIV-il WAR)
A civil war is a war between opposing groups of citizens within the same country. The American Civil War began in 1861.

compromise (KOM-pruh-myz)
A compromise is a way to settle a disagreement in which both sides give up part of what they want. President Garfield tried to reach a compromise with Senator Conkling over government jobs.

constitution (kon-stih-TOO-shun)
A constitution is the set of basic principles that govern a state, country, or society. As a lawyer, Arthur knew the U.S. Constitution well.

faction (FAK-shen)
A faction is a smaller group within a bigger organization, such as a political party. Factions often disagree with other members of the larger organization.

immigrate (IM-ih-grayt)
If people immigrate, they move to a new country. The Chinese Exclusion Act was meant to keep Chinese people from immigrating to the United States.

nominate (NOM-ih-nayt)
If a political party nominates someone, it chooses him or her to run for a political office. In 1880, the Republicans nominated James Garfield as their presidential candidate.

politics (PAWL-ih-tiks)
Politics refers to the actions and practices of the government. Arthur's interest in politics allowed him to share his beliefs with others.

protest (PROH-test)
If people protest against something, they speak out to say that it is wrong. People at the Anti-Nebraska Convention protested the Kansas-Nebraska Act.

scandal (SKAN-dl)
A scandal is a shameful action that shocks the public. Arthur continued Garfield's investigation of the Star Route scandal.

term (TERM)
A term is the length of time a politician can keep his or her position by law. Arthur did not run for a second term as president.

territories (TAIR-ih-tor-eez)
Territories are lands or regions, especially lands that belong to a government. Republicans were against the spread of slavery to new territories.

union (YOON-yen)
A union is the joining together of people or groups of people, such as states. The Union is another name for the United States.

veto (VEE-toh)
A veto is the president's power to refuse to sign a bill into law. Arthur vetoed the Chinese Exclusion Act.

Our PRESIDENTS

President	Birthplace	Life Span	Presidency	Political Party	First Lady
George Washington	Virginia	1732–1799	1789–1797	None	Martha Dandridge Custis Washington
John Adams	Massachusetts	1735–1826	1797–1801	Federalist	Abigail Smith Adams
Thomas Jefferson	Virginia	1743–1826	1801–1809	Democratic-Republican	widower
James Madison	Virginia	1751–1836	1809–1817	Democratic Republican	Dolley Payne Todd Madison
James Monroe	Virginia	1758–1831	1817–1825	Democratic Republican	Elizabeth Kortright Monroe
John Quincy Adams	Massachusetts	1767–1848	1825–1829	Democratic-Republican	Louisa Johnson Adams
Andrew Jackson	South Carolina	1767–1845	1829–1837	Democrat	widower
Martin Van Buren	New York	1782–1862	1837–1841	Democrat	widower
William H. Harrison	Virginia	1773–1841	1841	Whig	Anna Symmes Harrison
John Tyler	Virginia	1790–1862	1841–1845	Whig	Letitia Christian Tyler Julia Gardiner Tyler
James K. Polk	North Carolina	1795–1849	1845–1849	Democrat	Sarah Childress Polk

President	Birthplace	Life Span	Presidency	Political Party	First Lady
Zachary Taylor	Virginia	1784–1850	1849–1850	Whig	Margaret Mackall Smith Taylor
Millard Fillmore	New York	1800–1874	1850–1853	Whig	Abigail Powers Fillmore
Franklin Pierce	New Hampshire	1804–1869	1853–1857	Democrat	Jane Means Appleton Pierce
James Buchanan	Pennsylvania	1791–1868	1857–1861	Democrat	never married
Abraham Lincoln	Kentucky	1809–1865	1861–1865	Republican	Mary Todd Lincoln
Andrew Johnson	North Carolina	1808–1875	1865–1869	Democrat	Eliza McCardle Johnson
Ulysses S. Grant	Ohio	1822–1885	1869–1877	Republican	Julia Dent Grant
Rutherford B. Hayes	Ohio	1822–1893	1877–1881	Republican	Lucy Webb Hayes
James A. Garfield	Ohio	1831–1881	1881	Republican	Lucretia Rudolph Garfield
Chester A. Arthur	Vermont	1829–1886	1881–1885	Republican	widower
Grover Cleveland	New Jersey	1837–1908	1885–1889	Democrat	Frances Folsom Cleveland

Our PRESIDENTS

	President	Birthplace	Life Span	Presidency	Political Party	First Lady
	Benjamin Harrison	Ohio	1833–1901	1889–1893	Republican	Caroline Scott Harrison
	Grover Cleveland	New Jersey	1837–1908	1893–1897	Democrat	Frances Folsom Cleveland
	William McKinley	Ohio	1843–1901	1897–1901	Republican	Ida Saxton McKinley
	Theodore Roosevelt	New York	1858–1919	1901–1909	Republican	Edith Kermit Carow Roosevelt
	William H. Taft	Ohio	1857–1930	1909–1913	Republican	Helen Herron Taft
	Woodrow Wilson	Virginia	1856–1924	1913–1921	Democrat	Ellen L. Axson Wilson / Edith Bolling Galt Wilson
	Warren G. Harding	Ohio	1865–1923	1921–1923	Republican	Florence Kling De Wolfe Harding
	Calvin Coolidge	Vermont	1872–1933	1923–1929	Republican	Grace Goodhue Coolidge
	Herbert C. Hoover	Iowa	1874–1964	1929–1933	Republican	Lou Henry Hoover
	Franklin D. Roosevelt	New York	1882–1945	1933–1945	Democrat	Anna Eleanor Roosevelt Roosevelt
	Harry S. Truman	Missouri	1884–1972	1945–1953	Democrat	Elizabeth Wallace Truman

Our PRESIDENTS

President	Birthplace	Life Span	Presidency	Political Party	First Lady
Dwight D. Eisenhower	Texas	1890–1969	1953–1961	Republican	Mary "Mamie" Doud Eisenhower
John F. Kennedy	Massachusetts	1917–1963	1961–1963	Democrat	Jacqueline Bouvier Kennedy
Lyndon B. Johnson	Texas	1908–1973	1963–1969	Democrat	Claudia Alta Taylor Johnson
Richard M. Nixon	California	1913–1994	1969–1974	Republican	Thelma Catherine Ryan Nixon
Gerald Ford	Nebraska	1913–	1974–1977	Republican	Elizabeth "Betty" Bloomer Warren Ford
James Carter	Georgia	1924–	1977–1981	Democrat	Rosalynn Smith Carter
Ronald Reagan	Illinois	1911–	1981–1989	Republican	Nancy Davis Reagan
George Bush	Massachusetts	1924–	1989–1993	Republican	Barbara Pierce Bush
William Clinton	Arkansas	1946–	1993–2001	Democrat	Hillary Rodham Clinton
George W. Bush	Connecticut	1946–	2001–	Republican	Laura Welch Bush

Qualifications

To run for president, a candidate must
- be at least 35 years old
- be a citizen who was born in the United States
- have lived in the United States for 14 years

Term of Office

A president's term of office is four years. No president can stay in office for more than two terms.

Election Date

The presidential election takes place every four years on the first Tuesday of November.

Inauguration Date

Presidents are inaugurated on January 20.

Oath of Office

I do solemnly swear I will faithfully execute the office of the President of the United States and will to the best of my ability preserve, protect, and defend the Constitution of the United States.

Write a Letter to the President

One of the best things about being a U.S. citizen is that Americans get to participate in their government. They can speak out if they feel government leaders aren't doing their jobs. They can also praise leaders who are going the extra mile. Do you have something you'd like the president to do? Should the president worry more about the environment and encourage people to recycle? Should the government spend more money on our schools? You can write a letter to the president to say how you feel!

1600 Pennsylvania Avenue
Washington, D.C. 20500

You can even send an e-mail to: president@whitehouse.gov

For Further INFORMATION

Internet Sites

Read encyclopedia entries about Chester A. Arthur:
http://gi.grolier.com/presidents/ea/bios/21parth.html
http://encarta.msn.com/index/conciseindex/44/0444A000.htm

Learn more about Chester Arthur at the Discovery Channel site:
http://school.discovery.com/students/homeworkhelp/worldbook/atozhistory/a/032240.html

Visit the Irish ancestral home of Arthur's father:
http://www.antrim.net/Cullybackey/authur/Arthur_Cottage.htm

Visit President Arthur's childhood home in Vermont:
http://www.cit.state.vt.us/dca/historic/hp_sites.htm

Learn more about all the presidents and visit the White House:
http://www.whitehouse.gov/WH/glimpse/presidents/html/presidents.html
http://www.thepresidency.org/presinfo.htm
http://www.americanpresidents.org/

Books

Brunelli, Carol. *James Garfield: Our Twentieth President.* Chanhassen, MN:
The Child's World, 2002.

Francis, Sandra. *Rutherford B. Hayes: Our Nineteenth President.* Chanhassen, MN:
The Child's World, 2002.

Simon, Charnon. *Chester A. Arthur: Twenty-First President of the United States
(Encyclopedia of Presidents).* Chicago: Childrens Press, 1989.

Stevens, Rita. *Chester A. Arthur: 21st President of the United States.* Ada, OK:
Garrett Educational, 1988.

Index

ABCD ships, 33
abolitionists, 8
African Americans, rights of, 11-12, 38
Anti-Nebraska Convention, 11, 13
Arthur, Chester
  birth of, 8, 38
  campaigning work, 12-13, 15, 38-39
  as customs collector, 18-21, 23, 24, 39
  death of, 37, 39
  education of, 9, 38
  honesty of, 28-29
  illness of, 35-37, 39
  law practice, 10-12, 14, 16, 38
  marriage of, 14, 38
  navy, rebuilding of, 32-34, 39
  as president, 26-36, 39
  public opinion of, 33, 35
  as quartermaster general, 16-17, 38
  veto power, 34, 35
  as vice president, 24-26, 39
  as vice presidential candidate, 21-24, 39
Arthur, Chester Alan Jr., 14
Arthur, Ellen (daughter), 14
Arthur, Ellen (wife), 14, 16, 21-22, 39
Arthur, Malvina, 7-8, 38
Arthur, William, 7-9, 38

Bell, Alexander Graham, 31
Blaine, James G., 37, 39
Bovay, Alan Earl, 13
Brady, Thomas, 29
Bright's disease, 35, 37, 39

Chinese Exclusion Act, 34-35, 39
civil rights, 11-12, 34
Civil Service Commission, 29-30
Civil War, 16, 32, 38-39
Cleveland, Grover, 37, 39
Conkling, Roscoe, 16-17, 19, 21, 24-27, 38
Coolidge, Calvin, 6, 7
Culver, Erastus D., 10-12, 38

Democratic Party, 13
Democratic-Republican Party, 13

Fillmore, Millard, 26, 30
Fremont, John C., 12-13

Garfield, James, 7, 11, 21-22, 23-29, 31, 39
Grant, Ulysses S., 18, 39
Guiteau, Charles J., 26-27

Harding, Warren, 7
Hayes, Rutherford B., 19-21, 23, 26, 39
Herndon, Ellen. See Arthur, Ellen (wife)

immigration, 34-35

Jefferson, Thomas, 13
Jennings, Lizzie, 11-12, 38
Johnson, Andrew, 26, 30

Kansas-Nebraska Act, 11, 13

Lemmon, Jonathan, 12, 38
Lincoln, Abraham, 13, 15-16, 26, 27, 38
Lincoln, Robert T., 27

McElvoy, Mary Arthur, 28
merit system, 23, 29
Morgan, Edwin D., 15-16, 38

Native Americans, 27
Naval War College, 33
Navy Bill, 32, 33
New York Anti-Slavery Society, 8, 38
New York Customhouse, 18-19, 23, 39
Newcomb, Simon, 31

Paine, Elijah, 12
patronage, 18-20, 23-25
Pendleton Act, 29-30, 39

Republican Party, 11-13, 16, 18-21, 23, 25, 28,
  30, 38, 39

Seymour, Horatio, 16
slavery, 8-11, 13, 16, 38
Stalwarts, 16, 18-19, 23-29, 38-39
Star Route scandal, 28-29
Stone, Malvina. See Arthur, Malvina

Twain, Mark, 35
Tyler, John, 26, 30

Union College, 9, 11, 38
U.S. Navy, 32-34, 39
U.S. Postal Service scandal, 28-29

Whig Party, 13
White House, 35

jB
ARTHUR

Brunelli, Carol.

Chester A. Arthur.

$27.07

DATE			

JAN - 7 2003